Stop! Don't step on that rock!

Pick it up and look at it instead. The rock in your hand may be millions of years old! If it could talk, the rock might tell you that it was once part of a magnificent mountain or part of a cave dweller's home. Maybe it was trampled on by a dinosaur!

But the rock doesn't have to talk to reveal its history. You can tell a lot about a rock just by looking at it closely. There are also several simple tests that can help identify a rock or mineral. So, if you want to be a rock hound, read on! This book will help you discover the fascinating world of rocks and minerals and show you how to start building your own rock and mineral collections.

What are rocks and minerals?

Most rocks, but not all, are made up of minerals. Minerals are elements or compounds that (1) are found naturally in the earth and (2) are not living things. This means that substances like nylon or plastic, which are human-made, are not minerals. It also means that bones, shells, and wood are not minerals because they are parts of living things.

Every mineral has a definite chemical composition and a crystalline structure. A rock, on the other hand, may be a combination of several different minerals or a mixture of minerals and nonminerals.

Rocks are identified by such properties as color, texture, mineral composition, and grain. The table on page 3 shows a few of the general characteristics of some common rocks.

General Properties of Common Rocks

NAME OF ROCK	COMPOSITION	COLOR	GRAIN SIZE
Granite	quartz, feldspar, mica	gray to pink	coarse
Sandstone	quartz, limonite, calcite	varied (yellowish, pink, brown, or other)	varied
Conglomerate	pebbles, gravel, sand, various minerals	mostly gray	large inclusions
Shale	hardened mud, clay (layered)	gray (dull)	fine
Limestone	calcite (from shells of tiny sea animals)	gray, white, black	varied
Gneiss	formed from any type of rock	banded (colors vary)	coarse
Slate	formed from shale	gray and other colors (shiny luster)	fine

CONGLOMERATE ROCK WITH PEBBLES

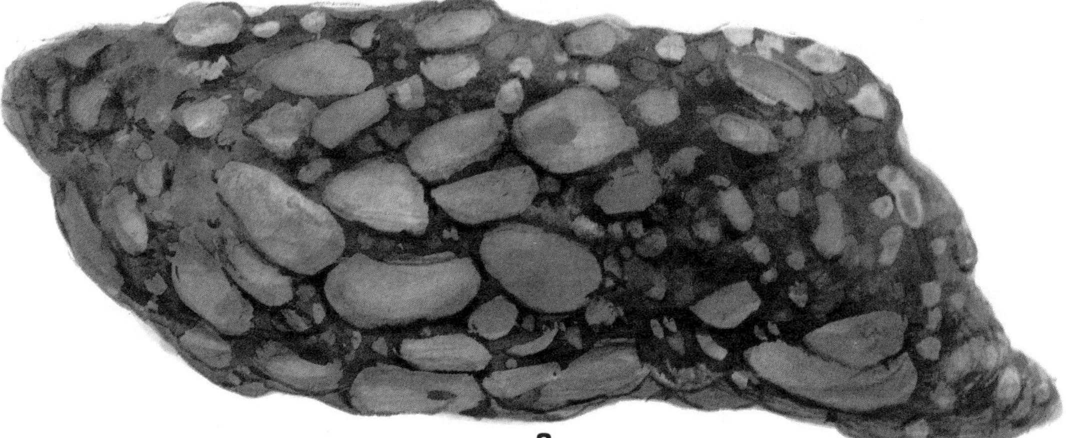

Are there different types of rocks?

All rocks are not the same, which is why a rock collection is so interesting. There are three basic types of rocks: *igneous*, *sedimentary*, and *metamorphic*. How a rock is formed determines what type of rock it will be.

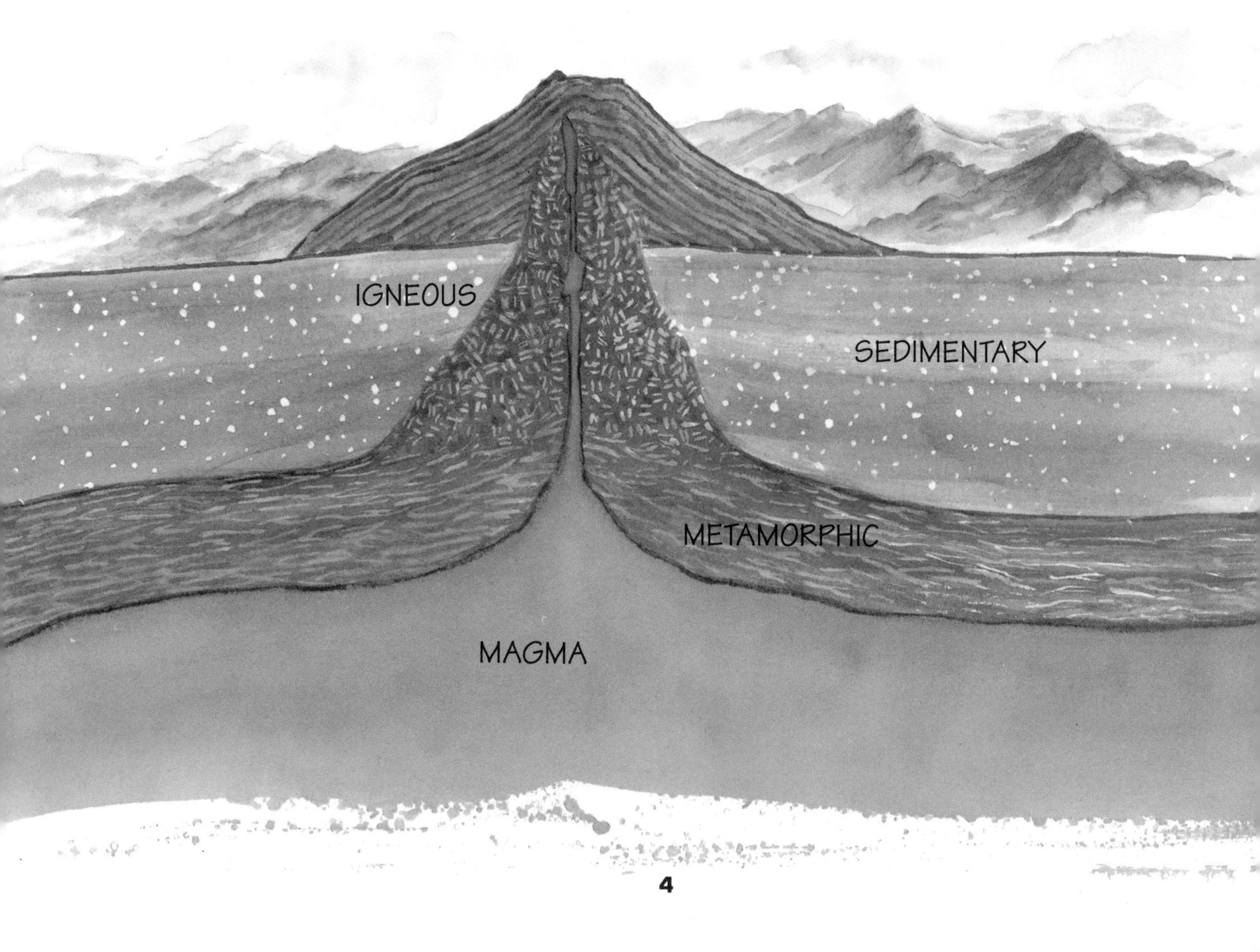

PEGMATITE

OBSIDIAN

How are igneous rocks formed?

Deep inside the earth, the temperature is very high. It is so high, in fact, that minerals within the earth are in liquid form and are called *magma*. As the magma rises toward the earth's surface, it starts to cool. When the magma is cool enough, it turns into solid *igneous* rock. This may happen beneath the earth or when the liquid rock, known as *lava*, reaches the surface.

If the rock cools slowly, the minerals in it can form crystals. A slow-cooling rock such as pegmatite can contain giant crystals that are up to several feet long. Because basalt cools fairly quickly, the crystals it contains are very small. Obsidian, a rock that forms when a volcano erupts and molten rock is suddenly exposed to air, is an example of a fast-cooling rock. It has no crystals at all and looks like smooth black glass.

How are sedimentary rocks formed?

The earth's surface is constantly being *eroded*, or broken up into smaller pieces by wind and water. The small pieces of rock tumble down rivers and streams. Also, especially during ice ages, glaciers drag tons of rock across the land. Over time, as layers and layers of rock fragments are deposited, the pieces become pressed together and form solid rock. Because of the way it is formed, *sedimentary* rock is found in layers.

Wonderstone is an example of a sedimentary rock called sandstone. Conglomerate is a type of sedimentary rock that contains rounded pebbles, while breccia has sharp-edged pebbles. Limestone is another example of a sedimentary rock. It is made from tiny pieces of shell or coral.

Shale is a sedimentary rock that is made of finely ground grains of mud or clay. Because it is quite soft, its layers can be easily separated with a pocket knife. If you are lucky, you will find a surprise inside—the perfect imprint of a leaf or the bony skeleton of an insect or fish that lived millions of years ago. After the plant or animal died, it was covered with sediment that hardened into rock. After a long time, the once-living matter disintegrated and minerals filled up the space. The imprint that remains is called a *fossil*. Petrified wood, which was once wood and is now rock, is another example of a fossil.

How are metamorphic rocks formed?

Metamorphic comes from the Greek words *meta*, meaning change, and *morphe*, meaning form. A metamorphic rock is one that was igneous or sedimentary but has undergone a complete change to become a new and different rock. Rocks change form when they are exposed to tremendous heat or pressure. These conditions occur when large sections of the earth's crust move toward each other and collide, and tons and tons of rock pile up on top of each other. The pressure from so much weight heats up the buried rock, causing the minerals and nonminerals in the rock to change form. At other times, melted rock beneath the earth's surface is forced up through cracks. The heat from the melted rock causes nearby rocks to change form.

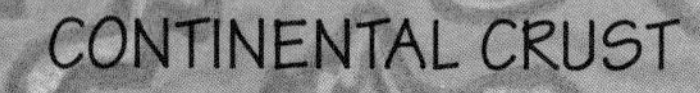

Quartzite is an example of a metamorphic rock. It was originally sandstone. Slate is formed from shale; and marble was once limestone.

As you can see, rocks come in three forms and can be made up of many combinations of minerals and nonminerals. Collecting them can be fun.

What tools do I need for rock and mineral collecting?

You will need to gather these basic tools before you begin. You should be able to buy these items at a hardware store or from a rock and mineral dealer.

- **ROCK HAMMER**—with a square head and a pointed end for breaking off small rock specimens to take home.
- **CHISEL**—a good tool for loosening mineral crystals.
- **POCKET KNIFE**—to dig out any fossils you may find and to test the hardness of minerals.
- **MAGNIFYING GLASS**—to take a closer look at the different mineral crystals or other structures in each type of rock.
- **SMALL LABELS**—to label each rock specimen (name, where you found it, etc.).
- **NOTEBOOK AND PENCIL**—to jot down notes about the date and the area where you found your specimens.
- **NEWSPAPER**—to wrap each specimen in so that the rocks don't hit against one another and break.
- **STRONG CANVAS BAG**—for carrying your finds home.
- **SHIRT BOX TOPS OR BOTTOMS AND SMALL PLASTIC BAGS**—for cataloging and storing your specimens by category (rocks or minerals) and type.

Where should I look for specimens?

Now that you have everything you need for rock hunting, where should you go? Look for places where there is exposed rock, such as stream beds, hillside ledges, and road cuts. *Be careful while you are looking for specimens. Let someone know where you will be exploring and take along a friend. If you know you will be collecting specimens on someone's private property, ask permission before you begin.*

Identifying the rocks and minerals you find is like solving a mystery! You have to look for clues. A good handbook with color photos of rocks and minerals will help you follow up on hunches. So will doing some simple tests on the specimens you find.

What clues will help me identify rocks and minerals?

Imagine you are rock hunting and you find a large crystal of a mineral. How can you identify it? One clue is *color*, although different specimens of the same mineral may have slightly different colors. A good way to determine true color is with a *streak test*. To perform the test, find a piece of old or discarded ceramic tile and scrape an edge of your crystal on the unglazed side of the tile. The powder the mineral leaves on the tile is its true color. Pyrite, for example, is often called "fool's gold" because it has a golden shine. But if you do a streak test on pyrite, you'll see that it leaves a black streak.

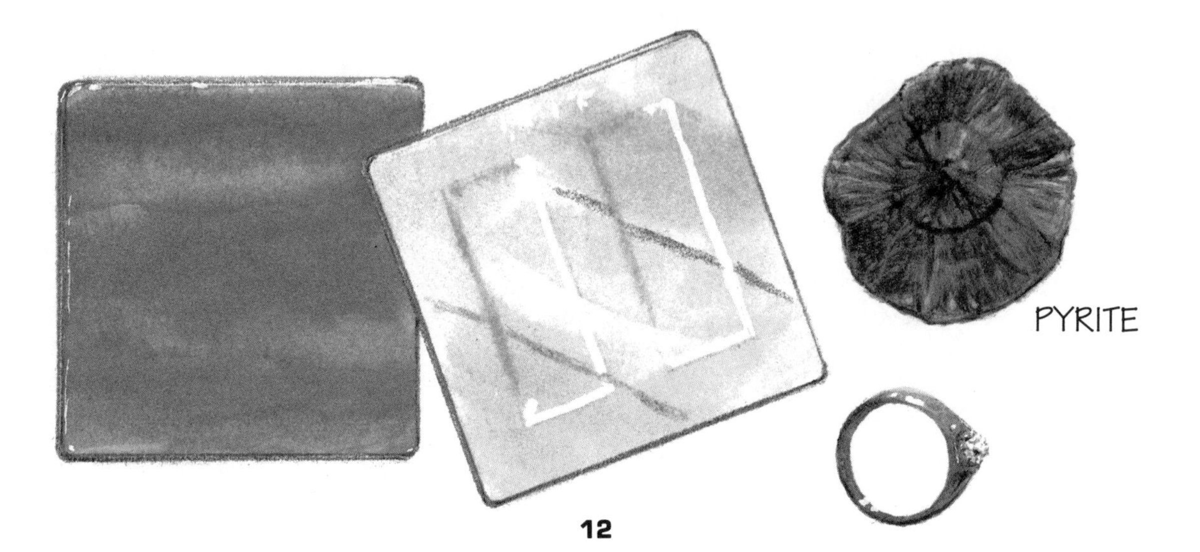

Another property of minerals is *luster*. Luster is the way a mineral shines when light hits its surface. Minerals can be metallic like gold and galena, glassy like quartz, pearly like talc, sparkling like a diamond, or dull like kaolinite (the mineral in clay). Luster will also help you identify your specimen.

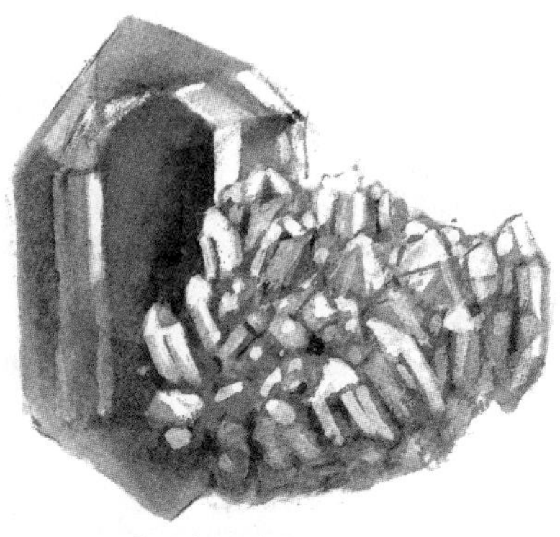

QUARTZ

DIAMOND

KAOLINITE

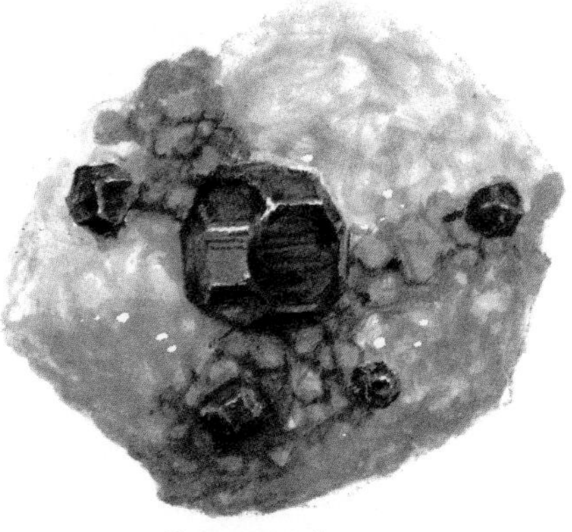

GALENA

Minerals have different degrees of *hardness*, or resistance to scratching. Talc and gypsum are so soft you can scratch them with your fingernail. A piece of quartz will scratch feldspar. Diamond, the hardest mineral, will scratch all common minerals. The table below, called the *Mohs scale*, measures a mineral's hardness from 1 to 10, with 1 being the softest.

MOHS SCALE OF HARDNESS

1 TALC

2 GYPSUM

3 CALCITE

4 FLUORITE

5 APATITE

6 FELDSPAR

7 QUARTZ

8 TOPAZ

9 CORUNDUM

10 DIAMOND

Many minerals will break in a special way called *cleavage*. These minerals break in a certain direction with a smooth plane. Mica, for example, breaks into thin sheets with flat surfaces. Other minerals *fracture*, or have irregular breaks. The breaks in obsidian are called *conchoidal*. They are curved like the inside of a shell.

The way a mineral breaks is a clue to its identity. Look carefully for this and other clues, and you'll soon be able to identify all of the rocks and minerals in your collection.

GRAPHITE

Here's a checklist of some minerals and their properties. Look for these same properties in the specimens you find, and you'll be well on your way to building a fine rock and mineral collection of your very own.

GOLD/ QUART

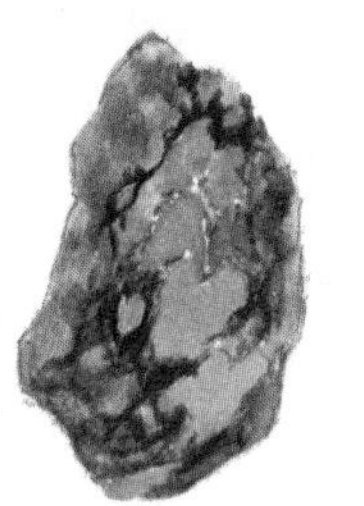

TURQUOISE

MINERAL	COLOR	STREAK	LUSTER	HARDNESS	OTHER PROPERTIES
Graphite	black	black	metallic	1	crystals are rare
Mica	colorless	white	pearly	2 ½–3	flakes into sheets
Halite	colorless	white	glassy	2 ½	salty taste
Galena	gray	gray	metallic	2 ½–3	crystal cubes
Calcite	colorless	white	glassy	3	crystalline
Magnetite	black	black	dull	5 ½–6 ½	magnetic
Pyrite	golden	black	metallic	6–6 ½	looks like gold
Feldspar	various	white	glassy	6–6 ½	two cleavages
Quartz	colorless *	white	glassy	7	round fracture
Corundum	gray **	white	glassy	9	crystalline

* pure quartz; there are many colored quartzes

** pure corundum; small amounts of metallic impurities form rubies and sapphires

CORUNDUM (SAPPHIRE)

HAPPY ROCK HUNTING!

TITANITE